Smooth Pebbles
Pretty Shells

The Best Creative Writing of 2003

NAWG Publications

© 2003

ISBN 0-9546461-0-X

Published by NAWG Publications, whose Head Office is at:
The Arts Centre, Washington, Tyne & Wear NE38 2AB

Anthology edited, designed, illustrated and typeset
by Mike Wilson, Bridlington, East Yorkshire, for NAWG Publications

Printed in England by Jasprint Ltd., Washington, Tyne & Wear NE37 2SH

Contents

Introduction | *Mike Wilson* . . . . | 5
Foreword | *Hilda Slater* . . . . | 7
Best Free Verse Poem | *Dorothy Nelson* . . . . | 9
  Afternoon
Best Formal Poem | *Diane Impey* . . . . | 11
  Eating Songbirds
Best Short Story | *Irene Black* . . . . | 12
  Street Talk
Best Novel | *Lilian Ledger* . . . . | 16
  Our Lady of The Petty Thieves
Best Non-Fiction Article | *Pat Rowlands* . . . . | 27
  La Charrette
Best Sitcom | *Peter Rolls* . . . . | 30
  The Grass is Greener
Best Mini-Tale | *Catherine Cooper* . . . . | 36
  My Best Friend's Secret

Denise Robertson Silver Trophy for the Best Group Anthology .
The Friday Writers Circle 37
  A Galaxy of Rhyme and Prose

Judges' Comments
Free Verse Poem | *Stephen Wade* . . . . | 38
Formal Poem | *Alison Chisholm* . . . . | 39
Short Story | *Lynne Patrick* . . . . | 40
Sitcom | *Ken Rock* . . . . | 42
Non-Fiction Article | *John Jenkins* . . . . | 43
Novel | *Steve Bowkett* . . . . | 46
Best Mini-Tale | *Mike Wilson* . . . . | 48
Best Group Anthology | *Staff of The Arts Centre, Washington* | 49
The Full Results | . . . . | 50

Introduction

Message from the Chairman

Welcome to the sixth annual anthology of work from the prize-winners of the Creative Writing Competitions of the National Association of Writers' Groups.

Each year since 1998, the winners of the various categories in the annual competitions have had the pleasure of seeing their work in print. The first anthology was *Singing Rainbows*, taken from the title of Morag Hadley's first-placed short story *I can sing a rainbow*.

The following year saw *Afterglow*, its name taken from the first Afterglow event held immediately after the Awards Ceremony at the Festival of Writing that year. The Millennium anthology was *Pentryx*, while 2001's book was *Plums & Orange Peel*. The title was taken from a quote by Walter Raleigh, English lecturer and critic, 1861-1922: "An anthology is like all the plums and orange peel picked out of a cake."

New Anthology of Writing Gems summed up to perfection the essence of the new-style anthology in 2002. The year saw the first full colour cover on a perfect bound book, an enormous step forward in the anthology's appearance.

This year's title, *Smooth Pebbles Pretty Stones*, comes from Joseph Spence's *Anecdotes* on Isaac Newton: "I don't know what I may seem to the world, but as to myself, I seem to have been only like a boy playing on the sea-shore and diverting myself in now and then finding a smoother pebble or a prettier shell than ordinary, whilst the great ocean of truth lay all undiscovered before me."

It can surely be argued that the written pieces in this book represent those pebbles and shells, in that they have been selected by the judges as being "smoother" or "prettier" than other entries.

Enjoy reading the best work by the members of our association.

Mike Wilson

Foreword

Message from the Competition Administrator

Who would have thought that as I write this piece for the anthology containing last year's winning competition entries, I would already have received the first of this year's entries. So congratulations to the early birds and good luck; maybe next year you will be in an anthology like this one.

This book contains the best of a lot of excellent work and from these chosen pieces you can gauge how high the standard was and how stiff the competition. I hope that if you were not a winner you will realise what an accolade it is to be amongst the winners and that you will be spurred on to enter the current competition and to appear in next year's anthology.

Meantime to those of you whose work does appear here "Congratulations." Isn't it a good feeling to see your work so well presented, for which we have to thank Mike, who puts it all together so well.

Having said all that, you can see that I have nothing here to take credit for. You do the work, the judges judge and Mike puts the result together in a lovely book. I am just here to say thank you to all of the above and I now move on to concentrate on the new competition.

Thank you all.

Hilda Slater
Competition Administrator 2003/4

Best Free Verse Poem
Judged by Stephen Wade

Afternoon

I sit beside your bed with the clock ticking,
watch your blue eyes
gaze at the space between us,
and wonder if that light breathy sound
is yours or mine.

It is your bed breathing –
your airflow mattress joins us
in the wait;
sighs and soft breaths
pumped from a box
plugged in at the wall.

We too are plugged in,
locked in memory, love,
and the strain of holding on.
Today you seem not to be here.
Planning your departure,
are you, while I fill vacant hours?

Pheasants squabble over crusts on the lawn,
squirrels run beneath your window
and the sun streams in
to hold us in a dusty shaft.

I am here
separate from you and silent,
the guardian of our past,
clutching at stories recalled, recorded;
an itinerary of times shared
and things bought:

your cushions,
my childhood,
roses in a jug,
your remembered voice,
and a blue nightdress
I handstitched for you years ago
which I'd almost forgotten.

These things replace you now,
are what I have of you,
as afternoon drifts ticking
towards its end,

waits for a decision.

Dorothy Nelson
Ashton in Makerfield Writers & Literary Group

Best Formal Poem
Judged by Alison Chisholm

Eating songbirds

All hunters are like brothers when they meet.
Should not their gourmet tastes be satisfied
By eating songbird flesh that is so sweet –
Far sweeter than the trill before he died?
With sharpened knife to gouge the brittle frame,
and marinade of garlic, wine and oil,
What price the heart that fails to beat for shame
Of having lived to be the summer's foil?
What pride in being served as food for kings!
And what if they should eat his very soul?
He knows that though his voice no longer sings
His corpse has played a more important role.
    At heaven's gate he opens up his throat;
    In paradise there is no sweeter note.

Diane Impey
Market Rasen Writing Group

Best short story
Judged by Lynne Patrick

Short talk

Wide-awake now, I glanced at my bedside clock. Midnight. What the blazes was going on down there on the street? They were still at it, the two male voices that had smashed through my dreams.

'Get out!'

'Please . . .'

'Out! And don't come back.'

'But Dad, please . . .'

'Dad? I haven't got a son. Not any more.'

'Mum . . .'

'Don't you drag her into it. She doesn't want you here either. Just clear off.'

I couldn't help myself. Grabbing a jacket, I opened the balcony door and stepped out, feigning annoyance. 'How the hell's anyone supposed to sleep?'

I stared at the street below, my eyes gradually getting used to the gloom. A solitary sodium light outside the Salvation Army office opposite our flat projected an orange glow, softened by a wintry haze hovering over the pavement. Slumped against the wall was a young man, his hands covering his eyes, a scruffy mongrel at his side.

Something about him – the slouch of his shoulders perhaps, or his voice, chewed at the edges of my hard-won comfort.

Belinda called from the bedroom. 'What's up?'

'Some guys having a bit of a barney.'

'Come to bed. Nothing we can do.'

As always I surrendered, soon snuggling up to the warmth of Belinda's soft, scented flesh. My eyes began to close.

'Still here? Told you to beat it. And take that stinking animal with you.'

Sobs echoed through the darkness. 'Can't just chuck us out. Nowhere to go.'

'Think I care? Don't give a damn.'

I switched on the bedside light and nudged Belinda. 'They're at it again. Listen.'

'Sleep, Ed. Not your concern.'

Belinda was right. I should have covered my ears and minded my own business, but against my will I was caught up in the drama. A secret echo from my own past.

'Don't send me away, Dad, please. Not my fault . . .'

'Uh? Whose then? Mine and your Mum's, I suppose.'

No point in trying to sleep. I slipped on the jacket once more and went back out onto the balcony.

Apart from the dog, the young man was alone again, hammering on the Salvation Army door.

'Oi! Open up! Oi!'

Should I call down, I wondered, and tell him it wasn't a hostel, merely the Sally Army's local HQ?

I heard Belinda grumbling. 'Come back inside. Ed, I'm freezing.'

'You're cold! How d'you reckon that poor bugger feels? All he's got on's a tatty sweatshirt and jeans.'

The man gave the Sally Army's door a final kick, turned and stumbled across to the street lamp, the dog at his heels. Now I could see his face clearly. No older than seventeen. As if I were staring at myself ten years earlier.

Clinging onto the lamppost he started again; words directed at someone out of my range of vision.

'Give's another chance, Dad, promise . . .'

But it wasn't a voice from the shadows that answered. I watched as the boy straightened up, squared his shoulders and seemed to grow six inches. His face had lost its pathetic expression. Now it glowered into the distance and spat out words like venom.

'Promise? Hell you do. Bloody junkie. Had it up to here with you.' The boy jerked his hand across his throat.

Then he crumpled. He was the sobbing teenager once more. 'Nowhere to go. Scared.'

Belinda was calling again. 'They still at it?'

'Kid on a bad trip.'

'Come back to bed, love.'

'Think I'd better call the cops.'

'Cops aren't going to turn out to yet another bombed-out smack-head.'

Bombed-out smackhead. Yes that's what I'd been. Only if Belinda got an inkling, I'd be out. I felt sorry for the guy, but in some ways I hated him. I didn't want to be reminded.

The boy had stopped sobbing and staggered back to the Salvation Army doorway. He sank down in the open porch and huddled against the dog. Hell, it was no good. I had to do something.

'Haven't we still got that old blanket?' I said, slipping back into the flat. Belinda blinked at me through sleep-deprived eyes.

'Oh, somewhere – spare room. Ed – don't go down. Guy might be dangerous.'

'Can't leave him to freeze to death.'

'Stop being so melodramatic.'

'Bel, it's barely two degrees out there.'

'Loads of cardboard in the Sally Army's rubbish bins. He can help himself to that.'

I remembered: winter nights in shop entrances huddled in a cardboard box, passers-by uttering platitudes – *Cardboard's a very good insulator, you know; At least he's got the shelter of the doorway.* Sometimes they chucked a coin in my direction. I wanted to throw it right back at them, but I knew I needed it. You try it, I wanted to shout. You try spending the night on concrete, with the wind and the rain blasting in. You wouldn't think cardboard was such a good insulator if it was all you had.

'He can't help himself to anything,' I said. 'Too spaced out.'

I found a blanket in the spare room, pushing my guilt aside as I contemplated the empty divan. Every night in that lonely shop entrance I used to fantasise that some benefactor would whisk me away to a warm bed and a cup of hot soup, like a character from Dickens. Now I shunned the idea of inviting an unwashed druggie to crash out in my home.

Clutching the bedcover I closed the apartment block door behind me and stepped into the chilly night. I crossed the road and approached the trembling figure pressed into the doorway. He was on his side, coiled like an embryo, one arm hugging the dog, his face buried in its fur.

'Here,' I said. 'Take this.'

Slowly the face turned to reveal red-rimmed eyes, pupils dilated, lids heavy. They stared at me vacantly.

'I've brought you a blanket. Thought you might be cold.' Cringing at the banality of my words, I laid the bedcover across him. Then I turned away and hurried back to my apartment building.

'You'll never learn, big softie.' Belinda's arms tightened around me in the warm bed.

'Couldn't just leave him.'

'Guy probably brought it on himself, Ed.'

That's what they said about me, too. So what? If you're plumbing the depths of degradation, what does it matter how you got there? But it was no use arguing with Belinda.

A little later female voices penetrated my sleep.

'Look at that.'

'Yeah, another crackhead. That poor dog.'

'Should be a law against keeping dogs if you ain't got no address.'

'Too right. They only have 'em to con people into giving 'em dosh.'

'For flea powder.' They laughed at their joke, and moved on. Silence returned along with memories. How I'd longed for a dog, as I'd haunted my doorways. I'd envied those guys with a companion to keep them safe and never let them down. Then I got the chance at the clinic. If I could clean up my Dad might take me back. No place now in my life for a dog.

Next morning the sound of a siren ripped through the flat. I rushed onto the balcony to see an ambulance arriving. A Salvation Army officer stood by the boy's prone figure.

I raced across the road, still fastening my coat. 'What's happened?'

'Found him like this,' said the Sally Army Major. 'Don't know how long he's been here.'

'Since last night,' I said, staring at the still figure. 'Is he . . . ?'

A paramedic, who was attending the boy, looked up. 'Not yet. Don't know if he'll make it though.'

'What's wrong?'

'What isn't? OD'd – looks like crack – and a severe case of hypothermia.'

'But I took him down a blanket.'

'Oh, that was you, was it?' The Major said. 'When I found him it was tucked round the dog.'

Overcome by wretchedness I watched the paramedics hoist the boy onto a stretcher and wheel him to the ambulance. Then I heard a moan.

'He's coming round,' said a paramedic.

I went across to the ambulance. The tortured eyes were trying to open. The boy seemed to recognise me and struggled for words.

'Patch . . . don't let them take him . . . don't let them put him down.'

I glanced at the dog shivering in the doorway.

'It's OK. Don't worry about Patch.'

'Don't let them . . . promise.'

'I promise,' I heard myself say, 'I'll look after Patch. Till you come back for him.'

The boy found my hand and squeezed it.

'Do you want me to call anyone?'

He shook his head. Tears ran down his face. I remembered the tears in my father's eyes, when I arrived back on his doorstep, clean. But this boy had a harder battle to fight. For a short time last night he had become his father. No hint of compassion in that voice.

The stretcher slid into the ambulance and the doors closed.

I walked over to the dog and picked up the trailing lead.

'Come on. Patch,' I said. 'God alone knows how we'll explain this to Belinda.'

Irene Black
Guildford Writers' Circle

Best novel
Judged by Steve Bowkett

Our Lady of the Petty Thieves

This is a story about Catholics and shoplifting, set in Durham in 1997 the year of New Labour and Diana's death.

Tracey McFall has two young children and she is terminally religious. Her devotion to the Catholic Church and her bizarre house-keeping threaten to drive her violent husband, Declan, into the open arms and legs of Moyra Mason, a non-Catholic and a 38D cup.

Peggy Crawford, Tracey's mother, is 50. Years of chain-smoking and erratic eating habits show in her face. Peggy is resigned to her dysfunctional family but her constant worry is the removal (by Declan) of her three-year-old grandson, Thomas, who is her reason for living.

Rene Seaton, Peggy's close friend and work colleague at the Old People's Home, appears to have no such trauma. She is an organised woman who eats three square meals a day and has a seemingly happily married daughter.

The story tracks Peggy's quest to have her grandson restored to her, through trauma, crime, Tracey's unbelievable stupidity, and eventually an overdose, all running parallel with Rene's concerns for her own, very sick, daughter.

The dilemmas of the two women are resolved against a background of happy-clappy Tony Blair, Charles and Di and Dodi, and Di's subsequent death. It reveals the hilarity and heart-break of mothers and daughters and their conflicting values, all viewed through the rather jaundiced eyes of those august bodies the Working Men's Club and the Old People's Home, and all resting in the long shadow of the Catholic Church.

CHAPTER ONE

Saturday, 21st June, 1997, was Queen Elizabeth the Second's Official Birthday, and while the Monarch reviewed her troops in London, Peggy Crawford sat in front of the mirror at her local hairdressers in Durham.

'What shall I do with it this time, Peggy?' the girl ran her fingers through the wet, grey and brown hair.

'I like the way Princess Diana gets hers done,' Peggy ventured.

Although Diana was well and truly out of favour with the Royal Family, she still held a place in Peggy's heart.

'I'm not a magician, for God's sake,' the girl briskly brushed the snags out of the wet hair.

'Well then, a bit of back-combing and put plenty of lacquer on. I want it to look right for my birthday party. Fancy her running off with that Dodi.'

'Yes, fancy. She can't marry him, though,' Tina, the hairdresser, thoughtfully slowed down the attack on Peggy's hair. 'Even if he does own Harrods. He's a Jew.'

'No, he's not.' Peggy knew these things. 'He's an Arab.'

'Same thing, isn't it?' Once past the Church of England, Sunday School and the Nativity, Tina was on rocky ground.

'No it isn't. She'll not marry him, though.' As well as sharing a birthday with the Queen, Peggy was an authority on Diana's life and loves. She'd thought about the Queen just this morning, there was a clip on the telly showing men polishing brasses, grooming horses. Then all her own cards arrived. Flowers from Rene and Peter, a lovely spray with a card "Congratulations on your 50th birthday." Roses from Joe. Her daughter Tracey had given her a statue of Our Lady of Fatima. It stood two feet high and dominated everything in sight. 'It'll look lovely your sideboard, Mam.' Peggy wasn't sure. Tracey had also brought two brandy glasses, in a presentation case lined with blue satin.

Peggy had a feeling she'd seen them before, she thought they'd been presented to Declan for something or other.

Drinking for England, or something like that.

'Your feet look swollen, Peggy,' Tina observed.

'I'm breaking these shoes in for tonight. They're killing me already and I'm sitting down.'

Peggy eased her foot out of the left shoe and gratefully placed it on the cool ceramic floor.

'How many's coming to your Fiftieth, then?'

'God knows. I've catered for sixty, but there'll be plenty of hangers-on at the Working Men's Club.' Peggy took a deep drag on her Embassy Regal and blew the smoke upwards, watching it hang on the air above her reflection. 'I hope the bloody karaoke turns up.'

At seven-thirty that same evening Peggy and her best friend Rene Seaton, who worked with her at the Old People's Home, were sitting side by side, opposite Moyra Mason, the self-proclaimed femme fatale of the Club. Peggy wore a red blouse, a smart black skirt and the cruelly tight black patent leather shoes with a grosgrain bow on the front.

'Is that a new dress?' Peggy asked Moyra.

'Catalogue.'

'Makes you look fat.' Rene said.

'Doesn't,' Moyra protested, straightened her shoulders and thrust out her impressive 38D cup. 'I'm first on the karaoke.'

'Hope they're all a bit better than last weekend,' Joe, Peggy's husband, stood behind her chair, nursing his pint. Joe was a fine, hand-

17

some man in his late fifties, worried that Peggy might not enjoy the party, worried that it was costing a bomb to feed and water this lot, half of them free-loaders, worried that his leeks might have needed just a bit more watering when he'd rushed away to get ready for the party.

Declan, Peggy's son-in-law, had just arrived, leaving Tracey to settle the children and organise the baby-sitter.

'Brandy and Babysham, Peggy?' Declan shouted.

'Yes, thanks.' Peggy smiled, but only with her mouth as she made room for another glass on the table. Drinks were stacking up in front of every guest. A track-suited dwarf moved from table to table selling domino cards. Outside, the summer evening was heavy with rain, but inside all were chattering and drinking, determined to give Peggy a great fiftieth birthday.

'I sat and ate four Cornettos this afternoon,' Moyra confessed.

'Pig,' said Rene, 'no wonder you're fat.'

More guests arrived, friends and colleagues of Peggy and Rene from the Home, friends of Declan and Tracey, work-mates he and Peter, Rene's husband, had in common from the Tannery. Neighbours, relatives. Waitresses bustled about, organising trestle tables laden with quiches, pizzas, baked potatoes in foil, salads, cheese, pickles. The noise of conversation subsided to a steady hum as the compere of the Concert Room announced the beginning of the entertainment. One mediocre singer after another got up onto the stage. The performer before Moyra was singing, since she had changed her mind about being first.

'Get the audience warmed up a bit,' she conceded, downing a half of McEwan's Export with skill. The singer was a short, stocky man with one eye missing, leaving a bad scar, old stitches pulled together, a jagged white line across his face.

'He was gored by a bull, years ago,' Moyra volunteered.

'Should have gored his vocal chords,' said Rene.

'I'm next,' Moyra stood up, tugged at her too short, too tight white dress and smoothed her blonde hair. 'I'm doing *Stand By Your Man*, she reminded them as she walked to the stage.

'Stand by Your Man . . .' she warbled, dangerously close to the tune.

Her performance was not helped by the chief waitress announcing that the buffet was now ready. Chairs were scraped back as people began to queue, laughing and joking, drowning out the singer.

'Somebody should tell her,' Joe said.

'Tell her what?' demanded Declan.

'That she can't bloody sing.'

'Yes she can,' Declan would have none of it. 'And she's got a lovely figure.' Tracey returned to the table laden with three plates of food, one she handed to her father, one to Declan. Joe inspected the inside of his sandwich. 'This one's got stuffing,' he said. 'Anybody want stuffing?'

'Her on the stage, according to you,' said Peggy.

Two elderly ladies in identical grey two-pieces, their grey hair in the identical styles of an earlier time, stopped at Peggy's table to say happy birthday. One got out her compact and inspected her teeth, while the other fingered the upholstery of the Concert Room. 'These covers would just do my wheel-backs,' she said. 'They wanted £70 each in the Metro and that was after I had spent all that money on Kevin. Mind you, that was for everything. He'll never have to go through it again. D'you want the quiche?'

'Yes.' Tight perm number two retrieved her plate from her friend.

'Your Kevin's suffered, I'll say that.' Peggy leaned forward, conciliatory, in her best Care-Assistant-to-Old-Person mode.

'Is he still on the Zimmer?'

'No, only Paracetamol.'

Moyra returned from the stage, to desultory applause.

'Great that, Moyra,' said Declan. 'Wasn't she, Joe?'

'Aye.' Joe crammed another breadroll into his mouth.

Moyra didn't sit down. 'I'll grab my food and my handbag and go and sit with Cindy.' Nobody said goodbye apart from Declan.

Well wishers came and went with presents for Peggy, and a friend of Tracey's brought, as well as flowers for Peggy, a small gift for Tracey's new baby.

'Open it,' said Rene. Tracey unwrapped a small yellow fluffy duck.

'Oh, that's lovely,' Rene grabbed the toy, smoothed the soft down. 'Just the right thing to give a new baby. What're you going to call it?'

Tracey studied for a moment. 'Well, it's only a fluffy duck,' she said.

Rene had earlier been across to the table to inspect the pile of presents. 'Did Lily Watson give you that silver photo frame?' she asked Peggy.

'Yes.'

'It's the one I gave her for her silver wedding,' Rene sniffed.

'Who wants a drink?' Peter Seaton, Rene's husband, was in the chair.

'Mrs Johnson bought the other silver frame,' Tracey said. 'Is she still in the choir?'

'Yes,' Rene answered. 'They celebrate twenty five years this year.'

'Twenty five years,' Tracey looked pensive. 'It's a long time to be on your feet. Did you ever get that £2.50?'

This shorthand between the women was driving Peter mad. 'I'll say it again, then. Does anybody want a drink. It's my shout.'

'Brandy and Babysham, please, Peter. Are you flush, like?'

'Me? I've got enough to last the rest of my life. If I die before next weekend.' He wrote the rest of the order on the back of a cigarette packet. 'Shall I get one for Declan. He seems to have disappeared.'

There was an uncomfortable silence, until Peggy said. 'No, leave him out. If he can't sit with us, he can't drink with us.'

No sooner had Peter disappeared with the drinks order, than Declan re-appeared behind his wife's seat. Tracey wasn't enjoying herself so much. Feeding her new baby was proving difficult; her breasts were swollen and sore with painfully cracked nipples. Keeping Thomas entertained and almost potty-trained was becoming a nightmare of screaming tantrums. She had looked at the clock twenty times times between nine o'clock and nine-thirty.

'What's up with your face?' Declan demanded.

'Nothing.' Tracey answered.

'You look as miserable as sin.'

'I'm tired,' she said. 'And I have to get up for Mass in the morning.'

'Oh, I thought bloody Jesus wouldn't be far away. And don't say there's nothing wrong with your face. It's like my arse.'

Declan stormed away from the company and went to stand at the bar, his foot resting on the brass rail running along the bottom, his elbow on the counter, ordered himself a pint of Newcastle Brown. He was positioned strategically between his relatives' table and Moyra Mason's table. He talked to men who were also guests at the party, men from his blocking out shed at the Tannery, men he knew through the work he had done on their motor bikes, on their clapped-out old cars and a couple of men he would rather have avoided.

After the Club chucked them all out, the party de-camped to Peggy's home, the remainder of the buffet had been packed and transported with them and was now being handed around. Hugo Paterson, Rene's son -in-law, was doing his best to find some suitable music for the party. The musical taste in the Crawford household had not changed in years.

'My word, Peggy, this is all a bit old hat, isn't it?' Hugo's public school, Southern accent at odds with the rest of the shouting and carousing Geordie voices, as he picked up tapes of Abba, Nat King Cole.

'There's some Dean Martin,' she told him. Hugo ignored her, settled for Freddy Mercury. Peggy was in no mood to argue, wondering where Declan and Moyra Mason had got to.

They were still missing when the party ended at two o'clock in the morning.

CHAPTER TWO

'Can you you come over, Mam, I feel rotten.'

'Yes, I'll be there as soon as possible.'

Peggy put the phone down. If Tracey was as bad as she sounded, she certainly needed help with the two kids.

Within half an hour she had caught a bus into Durham, changed buses out of Durham and was walking towards Tracey's front door. The usual chaos of trike, Lego, brightly coloured plastic bricks, and a wooden push-along trolley to put them in, met her when Tracey opened the front door. She was still in her night-dress, her nose red, her eyes puffy. Three-year-old Thomas flung himself into his Gran's arms.

'Flu, is it?' Peggy cuddled the little boy, drinking in the warm, sleepy smell of him, surveyed her daughter over his bright blond head, put him down, took off her coat.

'You go back to bed, I'll see to these two. Tell me when to bring the baby up for feeding.'

'Oh thanks, Mam.' Tracey went straight up the stairs and Peggy followed Thomas into the sitting room. She had become accustomed to the shabby furniture, a couch upholstered in autumn colours which did not match the two armchairs, a dining table and four chairs in the further end of the living room, a mantel shelf dominated by bills, biros, a comb. New furniture didn't enter into the scheme of things in this house. Tracey knew better than to ask.

Peggy's day continued as it had started, in chaos, trying to entertain Thomas, trying to settle the baby after three attempts by Tracey to feed her.

'Why don't you put her on SMA?' Peggy asked. 'You're wearing yourself out, and she's not getting satisfied. New babies should sleep all the time.'

'That's what they tell you in the books,' Tracey replied. 'She hasn't slept more than two hours at a time since she was born.'

'Because she's hungry,' Peggy said, triumphantly. 'Put her on the bottle and she'll sleep the clock round.'

'If only.' Tracey sank back onto her pillows and sighed, reached for another Kleenex from the box at her elbow. 'Alright then, get some baby food at the chemist when you go shopping.'

Peggy needed no second telling. She saddled up both children, baby Katie into her pram, Thomas into his coat and shoes, made a cursory list, spaghetti hoops, chicken nuggets, yohurt, and "something for Declan's tea" hoping inspiration would strike as she stood in the aisles of Safeway.

At five-thirty, Peggy had settled the baby, trying not to say 'I told you so,' as she watched Katie gulp the new formula like a dying man, organised a game for Thomas in the garden, and was halfway through the evening meal for Declan when there was a commotion at the front door. She put down the pan she was carrying from stove to sink and stepped into the hall. Thomas was crowding the doorway, wailing.

'What's up?' she asked, as Declan followed the little boy in.

'He's playing out in his best shoes.' Declan's tone was aggressive. 'They were bought for him for the christening next month.' He cuffed his son around the head. 'Get upstairs, you useless little bugger.'

Thomas dashed upstairs to his mother, his wails now joined by the baby crying from her cot.

'Hang on,' Peggy said. 'I forgot he was still wearing them when we came back from the shops. He went to play in the garden and I've had more to do here, looking after this lot and cooking for you. You've got a bloody cheek, coming in here and complaining when I'm cooking your bloody meals. And, by the way, I gave Tracey the money for those shoes, if you must know.'

'So did I,' Declan shouted, stomping around the kitchen, rattling knives and forks on the draining board. 'But mine probably went to Father fucking Garvey for his bloody Church.'

'Nothing to do with me,' Peggy shouted back, raising her voice to match his. 'All I know is, I'm doing my best here and I don't need you coming in, bawling and shouting, and upsetting Thomas.'

The raised voices penetrated upstairs to Tracey's bedroom and brought her clattering downstairs. She was trembling with rage, her feet bare, her night-dress crumpled.

'What the hell is going on here, you two shouting and carrying on?'

'Nothing.' Peggy, seeing Tracey is such a state, tried to take the heat out of the situation. 'You go back to bed.'

'Bed,' Tracey shouted. 'Bed. That's all he thinks I'm good for. Bed and bloody kids. I'm not going back to bed. I'm going out. Time I started to have some fun, the way he does.' She grabbed at a matted hairbrush from its customary place on the windowsill and began attacking her long blond hair.

Declan and Peggy watched as she stood there, one hand on the ledge as though to support herself, fighting for control.

'Yes, out,' she shouted again. 'I'm going out. I must be bloody stupid to stay with him the way he treats you, when all you do is try to help us.'

Declan was beginning to wish he'd never started this. After a horrendous day among the stinking bloody skins at the Tannery, he was tired, demoralised. He re-acted the only way he knew.

Erect and belligerent, he shouted again at his wife. 'Shut your mouth and get back to bed or I'll fucking carry you. I can manage my own house without your fucking witch of a mother interfering.' Incoherent with rage, he could only resort to physical violence and raised his arm in the air.

'Don't you lay a finger on me,' Tracey shouted. 'You've done that once too often. And I'll not shut my mouth. I should shut my legs more often, that's what I should do.'

'Calm down, both of you.' Peggy stood with her arm around the shivering Thomas, who buried his face into her side. She gradually let him go as she reached for her anorak which was hanging on the back of the door.

'Don't go home yet, Mam. He's got something to say to you. He's going to apologise.'

'Me?' Declan picked up the *Northern Echo* and flung himself into a chair. 'I'm not apologising. But I'll tell you what I will say. I'll tell her now to get out and stay out. Stay away from here. She doesn't see those kids again. We want nothing to do with her.'

The two women stood facing each other across the cluttered kitchen, a pan of potatoes gone cold, meat drying up in the oven. Tracey's hair was no longer the sleek, golden curtain that Peggy was used to seeing. One side was sticking up wildly and the other half matted and sticking to her head with sweat. Her face was blotched with tears.

Fear tightened Peggy's spine. 'You can't mean that, Declan. You wouldn't keep me from Thomas?'

'It's useless trying to talk to him when he's like this,' Tracey said. 'Just go home, Mam.'

'But tell me he doesn't mean it. I've got to see Thomas.'

Declan kept his face buried in the newspaper.

'Just go home.' Tracey repeated. Peggy left the house, a sickening wave of misery engulfing her.

CHAPTER THREE

Peggy changed buses again in the City but didn't go straight home, not wanting Joe to see her so upset. She went into a cafe half filled with students and late shoppers, and ordered a Cappucino, embarrassed as the tears started again while she was talking to the waitress, embarrassed at the state of her red eyes. Uncontrollable tears welling up, unstoppable, like pee, or blood, she had no idea she could cry so much. She was tormented by her daughter's life, wanting to help, trying not to control, not knowing what to do for the best. Life was tough for Tracey with two small children and no help from Declan, Thomas screeching when he couldn't get his own way, potty training almost non-existent, now that Katie was on the scene. Peggy had planned to do so much to help in the next few weeks, taking Thomas away, with Joe to a caravan, having him to sleep over at her house.

She felt so useless, so helpless, more tears, flowing freely. Perhaps she was just run down, she told herself, perhaps she was working too hard at the Home. She spooned the melted chocolate off the top of her cup, tried to be rational, almost unaware of her surroundings, unaware of the bright asters in a slim vase on the white table cloth, the view across Elvet Bridge, a crane working high overhead on some new construction in the City. LAING in black letters high on a bright yellow crane. Domes and roofs, chimney pots in clusters of eights and tens.

The chatter of four Japanese people at the next table momentarily distracted her. They seemed to be arguing about the merits of buying one between four.

One what? Peggy was intrigued. One coffee? One chocolate chip cookie. Peggy half turned towards them, her irritation at her family transferred to the foreigners. She soon lost interest and returned to her agony over Thomas. She knew Tracey wouldn't condone Declan's action, she couldn't cope alone with the chaos, the relentlessness. Everywhere Peggy saw young mothers with two small children and often asked herself why they did it. Saddling themselves for the next twenty years at the beck and call of demanding children. And Peggy hardly dared confront the truth of Tracey's life style with Declan. And Joe was no help, telling her not to interfere, telling her that she made things worse by always being at Tracey's house. 'No wonder Declan gets fed up. How d'you think I would have felt if your mother had been here so much?' Peggy ignored him, certain she knew best. More tears at what she saw as Joe's unjustified criticism. Just like his bloody mother.

Two weeks later, Peggy's living room was filled with the smell of onions, drifting in from the adjacent kitchen, disturbing Joe's concentration on the *Daily Mirror*. She chopped and peeled as steak and kidney browned in the heavy frying pan, added more onions, mushrooms, flicked the lot around with a wooden spatula and then tipped it all into a deep casserole and put it in the oven. She mixed short crust pastry and slammed it into the fridge, pushing her hair off her brow with the back of her floury hand. Suddenly, she darted through the living room, past Joe, fluttering the racing pages of his newspaper, quickly dialled a number. Waited.

'Hello, pet, it's your Mam.' Silence. 'Well, I had to ring. Had to know how he's getting on. Did he have his meningitis jab?' Silence. 'Aha. Aha.' Silence. 'I've bought him a banana slide. It's here out the back. It's the one he always plays on in Early Learning. Always thought he owned it.' Peggy gave a nervous laugh. 'He used to push the other kids off.' Peggy gave a another nervous laugh, listened another moment. 'No it wasn't expensive. I can afford it. When can he come over and play on it?'

Joe folded his newspaper, came over to the phone, put his face close to Peggy. 'Leave them alone,' he mouthed. She clamped her hand over the phone.

'Shut up, you,' she barked. 'No not you, pet, your Dad.' Joe gave a deep sigh, walked out of the living room, through the kitchen into the garden.

'Yes I know what Declan threatened,' she continued, 'but you could bring him over anyway, bring him when Declan's at work, he'll never know.'

Silence.

'Well, you'll have to stand up to him sometime. I don't know what to make of you. I think you're on his side.'

Peggy banged the receiver down, marched back into the kitchen, dragged a huge stone-coloured mixing bowl from the bottom of the pantry floor, assembled flour, castor sugar, margarine, and opened the back door.

'D'you want a coffee cake?' she bellowed out to Joe. He looked up from the bottom of the banana slide, put down the spanner he was using.

'Looks like I'm going to get one,' he replied.

Peggy furiously beat sugar and fat, weighed flour, separated ingredients. Bloody Declan. Bloody bastard Declan. What if she never saw Thomas again. All her muscles tingled with fear.

By the time the cake was poured into two greaseproof-lined tins, her eyes were so blurred she could hardly see. She banged the cakes into the oven, and raced upstairs before Joe came in and saw the tears. After a while she dragged herself off the bed. Judging by the smell permeating the house, the cakes must be nearly finished. Her timer pinged as she splashed her face in the bathroom, and went down to rescue the cakes, golden brown, perfect.

She ran the tap over the washing up which she had dumped in the sink, switched the kettle on, made two mugs of tea and took them into the garden.

'Sorry I shouted at you.' She handed one to Joe. The summer afternoon was perfect, the sun bathing their small garden in warm soft light, the smell of damp earth clinging to Joe's hands.

'I've tightened that screw.' Joe sat on the end of the banana slide, mug in hand. 'He'll be safe enough now.'

'If he ever gets to play on it,' Peggy said, darkly.

'Course he will, Declan's just flexing his muscles and he's got a better chance of injecting some discipline into the lad, and some sense into our Tracey with you out the way.'

'How can you say that? I just try to help, I don't spoil Thomas.'

Joe said nothing, continued with his tea.

'Well, just the odd sweets. Hard lines if you can't spoil your first grandson. You don't understand, you've never had a baby.'

Joe put his mug down. 'He's not your baby, he's Tracey and Declan's.'

Peggy flounced indoors and began to make butter icing.

She had a very disturbed night, trying hard not to think about her family. Are all Grans like this, she thought. Norma wasn't obsessed about hers, adoring them but always complaining about the mess they made in Norma's perfect house. Norma could brag for England, Peggy concluded. But none of Peggy's friends had a daughter as dozy as Tracey. It took her till lunchtime to get the children organised and mostly that was with Peggy's help. She wasn't as quick as half her friends, Julie with the two-year-old, and whose insides hadn't knitted together after having the baby, Samantha who was on the edge a nervous breakdown, all of them complaining about the relentless slog of looking after young children.

'You'll look back on this time in a rosy glow,' Peggy had told them, loving her own time with Thomas, cuddled close to her on the couch, his skinny body against hers, his smell of chocolate and shampoo.

She checked that Joe was lying on his side, away from her, gently snoring and reached over to switch on the lamp, holding down the button to prevent the noisy click. Catherine Cookson's downtrodden heroine looked sadly up from the cover of the paperback lying on the bedside table, among a jumble of tablets, earrings, glasses. Two ragged children clutched at the heroine's Victorian skirt, another babe nestled in the woollen shawl at her breast. Peggy couldn't help thinking that, for a much-abused, penniless woman, she had beautifully permed hair and perfect make-up. She lifted her reading glasses off the table, turned to her page, reached out a hand to touch Joe's sturdy flank. He moved, gave a muffled fart, shuffled.

'Go back to sleep,' Peggy said quietly.

'Have to have a run-off,' he clambered out of bed, around the foot, his wind explosions becoming more strident, propelling him along the landing and down the two steps to the bathroom.

Peggy had put her light off when he returned and he climbed back into bed, displacing the weight. She lay towards him, needing comfort. Joe gathered her into his arms, burying his face in her breasts, and she held his shoulders, brushing her lips against the stubby salt and pepper flecked hair, tracing the lines of his brow, his neck, trying to obliterate the pain of her day.

Joe, gentle at first, then insistent, mounted her, fucked her competently, no frills, no small talk, rising to meet her needs, in a slow rhythmic dance they had perfected over the years. Afterwards she lay in the warmth and the wetness, the familiar, distinctive smell of Joe's semen, until he turned her away from him, cuddled into her back, his left hand tracing her soft round belly.

'D'you still want to read?' he asked.

'No.' She smiled in the dark. 'You could teach Tilly Trotter a thing or two.'

Lilian Ledger
Dunholme Writers' Group

26

Best non-fiction article
Judged by John Jenkins

La Charrette

O.K. So sit back. Get comfortable. Kick your shoes off. Get your glasses on your nose. Relax. The curtains swish back and reveal a wide screen. The lights go down. Sound surrounds you. You are at the movies. But not in one of those flash multiplex movie theatres. You're being transported back in time to a bijou theatre of a bygone age.

La Charrette is a tiny, cosy you might say, cinema that as its French name suggests was originally a wagon, an ancient disused railway wagon. And it is actually tucked into the back garden of an ordinary house on an ordinary street in Knightsbridge, a small town on the out-skirts of Swansea, South Wales. It has all the usual mod cons that every movie theatre has, it shows the latest Hollywood blockbusters as well as popular classics such as *Brief Encounter* and *Casablanca* – over and over again – and as you might have guessed has a very faithful following. This devoted band of friends and neighbours, all avid movie buffs, think it is the best movie theatre in Wales. And at 35 feet by 12 feet it certainly is the smallest.

It was the brainchild of Gwyn Phillips, who like all of us grew up fascinated by Hollywood and the magic of the movies. As a young boy of twelve Gwyn got a job delivering newsreels to several local movie theatres in Swansea during the second world war. His love of movies grew over the years and especially so in the heyday of the Hollywood music'als of the '50s. Films such as *South Pacific, Oklahoma,* and *Carousel* were the big hits of the day. Remember those?

Vowing to become the owner of his own movie house one day where he could show his favourite films, Gwyn saved enough money to buy two railway parcel wagons, costing £35, and converted them into one stationary building in his own back yard. When a local movie theatre closed Gwyn snapped up enough seats to fit his theatre. He decked it out with all the extras to make it comfortable and on completion in 1953 opened it under the name of La Charrette. Quite a grand name to people more used to the Odeon, or the Tudor (better known as The Bug and Flea), or the local Workman's Hall. But the name La Charrette caught on and is still here to this day. Almost fifty years later it is safe to say that for an old wagon with only twenty-three seats it has been a huge success.

It wasn't long before the La Charrette Film Club was formed by fans, friends and neighbours. It now boasts almost seventy members, all great supporters of the La Charrette ethos. In fact, the Club is so popular there is a long list of people waiting to join.

Brains are probably whirring now wondering how to fit sixty-plus members into a twenty-three-seater movie theatre. Well, it is all very democratically organised. Each member has his/her own seat for a certain night and pays no admission charge to the monthly presentations, only a £2 fee every month to belong to the Club. The members also have the right to propose or veto the choice of films. Showings are spread over a weekend from Friday to Sunday with the odd week-night for popular demand. Right now the favourite films are *My Big Fat Greek Wedding, Road to Perdition*, and for complete contrast, *The Pianist*, the story of the Warsaw ghetto uprising.

So, not only do the patrons get the pleasure of seeing all the latest movies, they also get to sit in comfortable splendour in tiered seats with completely unobstructed views of a wide-screen with the traditional red velvet curtains. This is no place for the more commonly devoured popcorn and ice cream. This is the world of the far more genteel tea and biscuits.

It was a big blow to everyone when in 1996 Gwyn suddenly died. His projectionist of twenty years, Wayne John, was left to carry on. Undaunted Wayne took charge. After all, the show must go on. He made a few technical changes to equipment to keep up with modern times but otherwise continued to run La Charrette as Gwyn would have wished. Instead of running two projectors, as they had in the past, changing the reel from one to the other every ten minutes, Wayne made it possible for the reel to be changed only every 30-40 minutes.

The latest development, thanks to a £6,000 grant from the Welsh Arts Council, has enabled Wayne to invest in a new computerised digital system using DVDs (digital versatile discs) as well as a new Dolby surround sound system.

While he also juggles a day job Wayne often takes the movie equipment on the road around Wales. He sets it up in remote village halls and brings popular movies to people who rarely get into town. This is somewhat reminiscent of William Haggar, one of the pioneers of the movie business in Wales. In the late 1800s Haggar took his Royal Electric Bioscope with its animated pictures, very often of his wife and eight children, around Wales with travelling fairs. He really started something.

By the 1920s, moving pictures, now in local halls, were so popular that they became the main source of entertainment for hundreds of people. They stimulated imagination beyond fever pitch. So much so that churches and chapels in Wales warned against this modern entertainment which could 'stimulate evil passions' and become an 'instrument of the Devil'! Whether 'the Devil made me do it' or not people have flocked to the movies ever since.

Already recognised by the locals in Knightsbridge as an essential part of their lives, in 1994 La Charrette received official recognition. The British Film Institute acknowledged the unique value of a movie theatre like La Charrette and it presented Gwyn with a special plaque.

It was fixed proudly to the newly built foyer at the side of the main building and unveiled by Kenneth Griffith, the well-known Welsh actor and film producer.

Plans are already being made for the 50th anniversary in October 2003 when at least a hundred faithful filmgoers will get together in the Baltic Inn for dinner to celebrate the life of Gwyn Phillips as the founder of La Charrette. They will also toast its continuing success and of course the genius of Hollywood for producing such wonderfully exciting movies that still stir the imagination. Just think of all the old stories that will be repeated over and over again that night!

So if you're ever in the area and can't get into the movie, pop into the local pub, Tafarn y Trap (Welsh for Tavern and Trap – as in horse and trap) and see and touch a more personal tribute to Gwyn. Here, pulled up to the bar, is a special director's chair sporting a brass plaque with Gwyn's name. Many a toast is still made in absentia to this marvellous man who has brought to his community so many happy hours of movie bliss.

Pat Rowlands
Carmarthen Writers' Group

Best sitcom
Judged by Ken Rock

The Grass is Greener

Background
The Crokers are a lively, one-parent family in conflict with authority –
and with a village community that automatically thinks the worst of
townspeople. Especially with an absent father serving seven years in
jail.

Mrs Croker instils honesty into the children, but is herself prepared
to sail fairly 'close to the wind' for the family's survival.

There are two strands to the story. The main plot-line (Croker
family settling into the village) is in self-contained episodes. The sub-
plot (events at Cotsmoor Prison) develops each week into an escape by
the gang. Ultimately, the family's good humour and energy win
through. So does honesty — but it is a close call at times.

Locations
Main settings: The Crokers new home: living room/kitchen/
bedroom/garden.
Also: Saxton Housing Department office.
Cotsmoor prison: Governor's office. Big Henry's cell. The
tunnel.
Cleech Magna Village Hall.

Main Characters
BEATRICE CROKER (40) (BEE). Cheerful and down to earth. Keeps
her family on the straight and narrow, while her husband, Arthur, is
'away.' Although, as she says, 'Honesty's a pretty plant, but it don't
always chew easy.'
CROKER CHILDREN. Connie (12), Didi (11), Edie (10), Fifi (9),
Gigi (8), Zoe (7), Ambrose (5), Bardolph (3). A strong family unit:
well-intentioned, although by no means angelic. Their interests
include insects, water, digging, zen, music (wind and drums) and
helping.
WALTER URQUHART, OBE (55). Director of Housing for the
Saxton Council. His staff seem to have difficulty with the Croker
case. He is going to sort it out.
COLONEL MYTCHETT (55). Governor of Cotsmoor Prison.
ARTHUR CROKER (40). Bee's husband. Getaway driver for Higgins
gang. Serving seven years.
BIG HENRY HIGGINS (50). Gang leader. Serving 12 years.
MRS BIG HENRY (55). Runs an informal 'aid society' for gang
members' families.

Outline of Six Episodes
1. House Hunting. Bureaucracy is hassled; a house is found. A trip to Cotsmoor prison establishes Arthur Croker and Big Henry. The family visit the house.
2. Moving in. The new house renovated. Croker house-warming shunned by village clique. Family revenge. Escape plot at Cotsmoor.
3. Village Fete. The Crokers help with catering and side-shows; fortune telling; the spelling bee. Tunnellers begin at Cotsmoor.
4. Private Enterprise. Crokers money-making for the Vicar: Universal Aunts; Neighbour Watch; anonymous letters. Problems at Cotsmoor.
5. Year of Culture. Crokers in cultural events: Art; dramatics. Witches' coven v. Vicar's exorcism. UFOs and other diversions at Cotsmoor.
6. Village Spirit. Best-Kept Village competition. Escape at Cotsmoor.

Extract 1. The Director of Housing is interviewing Mrs Croker
Int. Day. Urquhart's office
URQUHART: (LOOKS THROUGH DOOR INTO PASSAGE) Er, just a moment. There seems to be a crowd in the passage – some sort of school party.
MRS. CROKER: No, no, love. They're mine. Been in the toilets . . . They do like a toilet. (GOES TO DOOR) Come on, you lot – and mind you behave in Mr Urqu-Hart's office.
URQUHART: LOOKS IN HORROR AS SIX CHILDREN TROOP IN – DRESSED IN ELFIN UNIFORM AND WEARING BLACK BOOTS. THEY ARE SOAKING WET.
MRS CROKER: Good heavens, Crokers. You have been at the hot and cold, haven't you. Did you all wash your boots?
CONNIE: WHISPERS TO HER MOTHER.
MRS CROKER: (TO CONNIE) What's that, love? No towels? No drier? (TO CHILDREN) Well, don't just drip on Mr Urqu-Hart's carpet. Keep moving – spread it round a bit.
CHILDREN: HOP ABOUT, SHEDDING WATER.
MRS CROKER (TO URQUHART): D'you hear that? No towels – and the drier come off the wall. Shame in't it? You'd think a place like this . . . They do like a toilet.
URQUHART: Mrs Croker, we need your children's names. There's – er six of them, is that right?
MRS. CROKER: Oh, no love. The others is with the dogs . . . (TO DIDI) Didi, love, just nip and get Connie and Bardolph . . .
DIDI: GOES
MRS CROKER (SHOUTS TO DIDI): . . . And to bring the carrots. And mind them wheels!
URQUHART: No, really, Mrs Croker. No need . . .

MRS. CROKER: No trouble, love. The dogs is all right on their own –
well, for a bit anyway . . . But your Mr Harris – he didn't like the
dogs.

URQUHART: The names. Let me have the names!

MRS. CROKER: Well, there's Connie . . . she's 12 . . . and Didi,
you've seen her. And Edie . . . (BENDS DOWN TO THIRD
CHILD) . . . What's that, love?

EDIE: WHISPERS

MRS CROKER: She wants to curtsey for Mr Urqu-hart. She's in the
Fete, you see ...

EDIE: CURTSIES FOR MR URQUHART

URQUHART: Thank you -um, Edie . . . The names, Mrs Croker.

MRS. CROKER: Oh, yes . . . There's Fifi and Gigi and -er Zoe . . . I
expect you're wondering about the names – all alphabetical and
then jumping to Z . . . Well, to tell the truth, love, we thought if we
had a Z it'd be the last – a bit of a hint to Mother Nature, you know
. . . But somehow we went round again with Ambrose. And then
. . .

DIDI AND CONNIE: CRASH INTO THE ROOM, PUSHING
BARDOLPH IN A TROLLEY

MRS CROKE: (TICKLES CHILD): Ah, here he is – here's my little
Bardolph . . . We wanted to call him Baldrick – after the one on the
Tele – looked just like him when he was born . . . Lovely little red
face . . . But the Chaplain – he didn't think so

URQUHART: Chaplain?

MRS. CROKER: Yes, love. At the prison. Well, they wouldn't give
Arthur parole – not after the problem. So I had to get on to the
Bishop . . . He couldn't come hisself in the end, but it was lovely
. . . all Arthur's friends singing away . . . And Big Henry being the
godfather – nice of him weren't it? Well, you know, with him being
the Godfather and that . . .

(TO CONNIE) Ah, you got the carrots, love . . . Hand them round
then. And wipe a nice one for Mr. Urqu-Hart . . .

URQUHART: Not for me . . . Please let us get on . . .

CHILDREN: STAND IN A LINE, MUNCHING CARROTS.

MRS. CROKER: That's it, kids. Every scrap . . . no mess on Mr Urqu-
Hart's carpet (TURNS TO URQUHART) There, look at those
teeth. Don't you just like to see really healthy teeth?

Extract 2. The visit to Cotsmoor prison

Int. Day. The Governor's Office

COLONEL MYTCHETT, THE GOVERNOR, IS AT THE WINDOW
WITH HIS NEW DEPUTY. AT THE SIGHT OF MRS CROKER
WAVING, HE DRAWS BACK.

DEPUTY: A familiar face, Governor?

GOVERNOR: Yes, indeed, Mr Carson. All too familiar. Mrs Croker and her brood.

DEPUTY: Her husband . . . Croker? What's he . . . ?

GOVERNOR: Arthur Croker. Doing seven. The Cotswold Bank job. Keeps his head down, no problems in here. But his wife – well, best avoided.

DEPUTY: She looks harmless enough. Pretty smart, in fact. Eight kids and all . . .

GOVERNOR: Oh, she's smart enough. Talk her way anywhere . . . Believes in going to the top . . . Bishop's wife. Local MP. Chairman of Visitors. They've all had a basin-full.

DEPUTY: Persuasive, is she?

GOVERNOR: Donkey's legs, Mr Carson. Your predecessor would tell you. Tried to enforce 'Only two visitors at a time.' He hadn't reckoned on Mrs C . . . Joined him in church for Sunday morning service with eight sobbing children . . . Harangued him and his wife on splitting the family unit . . . Innocent souls adrift . . . They wept non-stop through lessons, sermon and prayers . . . unhinged the whole congregation.

DEPUTY: So you changed the rule?

GOVERNOR: Special dispensation. Now they have their own corner in the visiting area. As I say, Croker's harmless. The main thing is to keep Mrs Croker out of our hair . . .

Int. Day. Prison Visiting area

ARTHUR (WAITING. AS THE FAMILY APPROACH, HE SMILES.): Hello, kids. (HE SHARES OUT HUGS AND KISSES HIS WIFE.). What's this then. Bee? The dress and the flowers and that? All a bit haute de la cote, isn't it?

MRS CROKER: Well, perhaps. It just -er, turned up in a crate. On the doorstep. Funny, ennit?

ARTHUR (LOOKS HER IN THE EYE): Yes. Just one of those things.

MRS CROKER: How is Big Henry, then?

ARTHUR: Oh, he's fine. He's (LOOKS ACROSS ROOM) . . . Yes. Over there. With his wife.

ON THE FAR SIDE OF THE ROOM SIT MR AND MRS BIG HENRY. HER DRESS IS IDENTICAL TO MRS CROKER'S.

ARTHUR: Hmm . . . Her dress looks a bit like yours, come to mention it . . .

THEY SHARE A MEANINGFUL GLANCE.

MRS CROKER: Yes. Funny, ennit. Right, kids. Let's be showing your Dad your prezzes. And then you can tell him what's been going on. But first, we need to give him our Big News, don't we?

THE CHILDREN BEAM AT ARTHUR.

MRS CROKER: It's a house, love! At last. Out at Cleech Magna . . . Nice village. They're going to show us on Monday, but I've had a

quiet shufti already. Six bedrooms, plenty of garden. Nice big sheds
and -er, private, you know . . . Quiet lane at the back, too.

ARTHUR: Could be handy, then.

MRS CROKER: Could be . . . A bit of enterprise and that . . .

(TO KIDS) Anyway, come on kids, give your Dad's his prez.

(BECKONS TO WARDER) OK, general? You'll want to check this, I
expect.

CHILDREN: GIVE ARTHUR A PARCEL

ARTHUR: UNWRAPS PARCEL. IT IS A CHRISTMAS PUDDING.

MRS CROKER: WIELDS HER SCISSORS, CUTS UP THE
PUDDING.

(TO WARDER) All right, admiral? No hacksaws, no gunpowder. Have
a nibble.

WARDER: PEERS CLOSELY AT PUDDING. STALKS AWAY.

ARTHUR: (CAREFULLY FOLDS UP WRAPPING PAPER.) Thanks
for that, love. I'm sure it's just the job. Pudding looks good, too. . .
(THEY EXCHANGE GLANCES.)

Extract 3. The Visit to the House

Int. Day. Empty bedroom – Painted green.

THE ROOM IS FULL OF PLANTS, WRITHING UP THE WALLS
AND DECAYING ON THE FLOOR. A HUGE HUMAN EYE
DANGLES FROM THE CEILING. MRS CROKER STANDS IN
THE DOORWAY, HER EYES SLIT-LIKE. SHE SCREWS UP
HER FACE AT THE SMELL. HER FOOT KICKS SOMETHING
SMALL AND FURRY.

Ext. Day. Outside the front door

URQUHART AND HARRIS ARE WAITING.

MRS CROKER: COMES OUT AND LEANS ON THE DOOR,
LOOKING STUNNED.

URQUHART: Ah, Mrs Croker! That's it, then. Just a lick or two of
paint and . . .

MRS CROKER: This is demonic, ennit?

URQUHART: No, no, it's . . .

MRS CROKER:Yes, it is. D'you think I don't know demonic when I
see it.

URQUHART: No, I assure you Mrs Croker . . .

MRS CROKER: D'you really think I'm taking my nearest and dearest
into that . . . iniquity.

URQUHART: I can explain . . . Mother Earth . . .

MRS CROKER: You should be ashamed of yourself, Mr Urqu-Hart.
Never mind your OBE. I reckon you'll lose that, when I tells people
what you're suggesting . . . Satanic is what it is. Have you seen that
room up there! (GRASPS URQUHART AND DRAGS HIM
UPSTAIRS)

Int. Day. Green-painted room with Eye and dead vegetation
MRS CROKER: DRAGS URQUHART INTO THE DOORWAY.
URQUHART: BLENCHES AT THE SIGHT AND THE SMELL.
MRS CROKER: Mother Earth, is it? (SHE BIFFS THE EYE, PRODS
    THE FURRY OBJECT) One of your lost souls, I expect. I think
    we'd better have a little talk. Outside.
ALL EXIT.

Ext. Day. Outside the front door of No. 13
URQUHART, HARRIS AND MRS CROKER EMERGE.
MRS CROKER (CONFRONTS URQUHART): There's pentacles in
    the parlour . . . tentacles in the bedroom. The whole place is
    possessed, ennit? What else is there? I haven't even looked in the
    kitchen. Shall we . . . ? (MAKES TO RE-ENTER HOUSE)
URQUHART: No, no, Mrs Croker. Look, perhaps we should outline
    the case history. Miss Crabbe . . .
MRS CROKER: The previous . . .
URQUHART: Yes. Somewhat eccentric. Saw herself as a mystic. And,
    unfortunately, she didn't get on with the neighbours. She waged a
    campaign . . . tried to . . .
MRS CROKER: Cast spells?
URQUHART: No, no . . . Well, yes. She tried . . . nothing in it, of
    course . . . but she tried to focus, -er, spirits on her neighbours, the
    Cracknells . . .
MRS CROKER: Hmm. The Eye . . . and them arrows in the wall?
URQUHART: Yes, yes . . . I suppose so. But when the Cracknells won
    a million pounds on the pools . . . Well, Miss Crabbe just cracked.
    (LOOKS TO HARRIS.)
HARRIS: Couldn't take it.
URQUHART: Lost her way.
HARRIS: Saw the light.
THE CROSS-TALK IS INTERRUPTED BY THE CHILDREN,
    TRAILING PAST IN THEIR BLACK CLOAKS.
EDIE: Mum . . . Look what we found.
MRS CROKER: Not now, love . . .
CONNIE: In the shed. Mum. These little wax people . . . Look. Nice
    aren't they? (GIVES A WAX FIGURE TO HER MOTHER.)
MRS CROKER (HER EYES NARROW): Very pretty, love . . . OK,
    we'll be going in a minute. Nip and get the others into the bus. I'm
    just having a final word with the gentlemen . . .
URQUHART AND HARRIS QUAIL . . .

Pat Rowlands
Camberley Writers' Circle

Best Mini-Tale

Judged by Mike Wilson

My best friend's secret

I'm naked! Where am I?

As I woke, and came round, I started to remember. I was at Tony's.

Tony and I had been best friends since junior school.

Yesterday was Tony's 30th birthday, and we'd been celebrating into the early hours. Mark, my partner, worked shifts and had left early, encouraging me to stay and enjoy myself.

As the other guests left, Tony took my hand.

"Samantha, will you stay with me tonight?"

I hesitated, then nodded and smiled nervously.

We instinctively knew this would never happen again, or be spoken of. She leaned forward and gently kissed me.

Catherine Cooper

Best Group Anthology
Judged by the Staff of The Arts Centre, Washington

A Galaxy of Rhyme and Prose
by
The Friday Writers' Circle

A REVIEW

Peter Bibby ably and entertainingly introduces this Anthology with an extended metaphor built around the "galaxy" concept. The collected works move through various moods and subjects. Many of the best pieces are rooted firmly in the past, such as Grethe Dillon's *First Love* and Jack Wilson's *Absent Friends*. This story has a twist at the end, something The Friday Writers' Circle are particularly skilled at achieving successfully. *Her Only Obsession* by May Cookson and Gabrielle Street's *Talking Head* are good examples of this. Others entertain using humour especially Olive Holland and Thora Beddard with their poetry, and Walter Young with his wry observations on female life. Evelyn Mayers and Ornella Bushel are more reflective in their poetry, inviting us to share their experiences. I would have liked to see the two pieces entitled *Talking Head* given more imaginative titles, but overall this is a well-presented anthology of the best that writing workshop groups stimulate.

Sue Lozynskij
Bridlington Writers' Group
Winner of the East Riding of Yorkshire Poetry Competition 2002

Judge's report

Best free verse poem

I enjoyed judging the competition very much indeed, and the standard and variety here was very impressive. Most notable were the adventurous attempts to find unusual and striking subjects or themes, but there was also a heartening mix of seriousness, meditation and whimsical humour. My first shortlist comprised fifteen poems, and after that it became an uphill struggle to choose and find a rank order.

The poems submitted proved to be a showcase for the possibilities of free verse, with bold and creative use of tone, line-length and diction; in the end, the winning poems were chosen because they exemplify the strengths and emotive dynamic of free forms.

Stephen Wade

Judge's report
Best formal poem

It is always a delight to read a set of poems making contemporary use of those forms we have inherited from centuries of writing around the world. A good range of subjects was offered, and the only disappointment was the high proportion of entries excluded from the contest at first glance. These were poems which failed to observe the dynamics of their form, particularly with regard to metre; or were unfinished, lacking punctuation or titles, or the final revision that could have made them winners.

A strong shortlist of excellent poems emerged, and the final adjudication was difficult because of the fine quality of the writing. Prize winner or not, please accept my thanks for the privilege of being allowed to share your poetry.

First place: Eating Songbirds *(Diane Impey)*
This difficult and moving poem makes good use of the Elizabethan sonnet form. It is technically excellent, original and compelling. Many congratulations.

Second place: Superman *(Deborah J. Gotch)*
Witty, immediate and contemporary, this Elizabethan sonnet is, again, technically excellent. The sheer vitality of its language is a delight.

Third place: Checkmate (*John Statham*)
On the surface, this appears to be a simple, uncomplicated villanelle, but the layers of meaning emerge with each reading. The poet has moved the piece forward from one repeat on to the next, and made effective and unobtrusive use of the rhyming pattern.

Fourth place: Nicking Knickers *(Joan Condon)*
A deliciously wicked Elizabethan sonnet, this gives a comprehensive view of the key character and his wife in just fourteen lines. Rhyming is natural and unforced, and the wit is irresistible.

Fifth place: Secret Places
In this tautly worked villanelle the poet juxtaposes an idyllic scene with dark, menacing understones. The resonances remain with the reader long after the paper has been put down.

Highly Commended: Autumn Sonnet and Sweethearts Forgot.

Alison Chisholm

Judge's report

Best short story

The enthusiasm of the aspiring writer for the short story form seems to grow with the years: this year's NAWG competition attracted several hundred entries. It was a pleasure and an honour to be invited to select the winners – though I'm glad no-one pretended it would be easy. Choosing from such a wide array of style and subject matter was always going to be a complex and demanding task, and to all those who didn't make the cut I can only say don't give up; keep honing those skills and it might be your turn next year. And mine is only one opinion.

On my journey I encountered murder and drug dealing, laughter and violence, ghosts and memories (quite a few of those). The animal kingdom was well represented: dogs, dragons, monkeys, cats, butterflies, even a stickleback put in appearances.

If I'm honest I have to say they weren't all perfect. The most common of the problems I identified was a lack of resolution. Ruth Rendell once said that a short story needn't have a plot, but it should make a point. Sometimes 1 struggled to find one.

But generally speaking the standard was as high as I have come to expect from NAWG members. Choosing four winners and three commended entries was something of a challenge.

All seven were well crafted, with the page-turning quality that puts the joy into judging. They all had something salient to say about human nature, and they said it through sharply drawn characters in well observed situations.

The commended entries are:

The Perfect Fare *(Margaret Cronin)*: a tale of cynical greed which gets its just reward, told with a light touch and ending on a neat twist of fate.

Turbulence *(Eileen Dowsing)*: an original treatment of a familiar theme – near-death experience. It's poignant and well described, and makes good use of sensory experience.

Stickleback *(Joyce Reed)* stays in the memory for the characters. I do enjoy stories in which the reader understands more than the narrator.

And – deep breath, jump in, no going back now – in traditional reverse older:

Fourth: Priced Above Rubies *(Chris Barker)*. You could call it a sting. Lawyers might call it entrapment. I just call it a jolly good story, which drew me in and left me feeling satisfied.

Third: Spaced Out *(John Statham)*. Humour is always thin on the ground in short story competitions, and this made me laugh out loud. I shall remember Sam the four-year-old alien sideboard for a long time.

Second: The Gift *(Ghislane Davies-Goff)*. This sent me back to my Complete Shakespeare to check how the Battle of Agincourt really began. This author's version is a lot wittier!

And the winner is:

Street Talk *(Irene Black)*. No laughs here: just moving emotional truth that brought tears to the eyes of this hardened old hack.

Thanks you, NAWG. It's been a pleasure and a privilege.

Lynne Patrick

Judge's report

Best sitcom

Sitcom is probably one of the most difficult forms of writing. It was good see more entries this year but entrants should study the markets very carefully. Sitcom writing is very structured and you need to follow the format to succeed. Strong characters, fresh situations, fresh, funny, flowing dialogue will catch any producer's eye.

My thanks to everyone who participated in this very difficult category.

The result of the sitcom competition is as follows:

1. The Grass is Greener *(Peter Rolls)*
2. A House in the Country *(Sangie Sen)*
3. No Place for Heroes *(John Birch)*
4. Delusions of Darcy *(Lilian Ledger)*

Ken Rock

Judge's report

Best non-fiction article

Feature articles tend to be disregarded as an art form but they can be as difficult to construct as fiction and many of the guidelines for clear writing apply to most forms of prose.

Let's look at some guidelines which apply particularly to features aimed at magazines, newspapers and radio.

In most cases you have to write to length and if the prescribed length is 1,000 words, 500 or 5,000, it is no good if you vary by more than ten per cent. Every word must count.

You must learn the art of editing, of being a master of precis, and recognising tautology.

Remember that verbs are the engines of good writing. Good strong verbs without adverbs. If your piece is littered with adverbs it is a sign that your writing is weak.

Read through your work and take out all adverbs and improve all verbs where possible. While doing this remove all adjectives.

And, so, but. They can usually be deleted when they begin a sentence. I'm not a pedant insisting on strict grammatical control and perfect syntax. There is no valid reason why you should not begin a sentence with a conjunction but frequently they are superfluous. The same goes for *however* and *meanwhile* at the start of sentences. Replace only those adverbs, adjectives and conjunctions that are essential.

Have you varied the length of your sentences and your paragraphs? Remember that paragraphs which wander on for four or more sentences look fine on a book page, not so good in a magazine and worse in a newspaper.

While in good blue pencil mood have you checked for clichés and solecisms?

Did you construct your first and last paragraph at the same time giving a polished feel to the piece?

Take great care over your introduction. Never mind this widely accepted canard about editors being busy people as if doctors, dustmen and nurses spend all day doing crosswords and drinking coffee. Editors are no busier than anybody else but they have a formula for going through a pile of manuscripts which would make the average stakhanovite look like a malingerer in the Ruritanian army.

The introduction – the first paragraph – must make an impression. It must do it in about nine seconds.

Titles are important. Avoid labels. *Wine growing* is a label. *Growing wine in the Arctic circle* is better.

If you are using direct speech it should be clear who is speaking without excessive use of *he replied, she said* and other attributions.

Break up your narrative with vivid quotations. Edit out the dross and use the best.

Sometimes, as in a travel feature, basic facts are essential but they can interrupt the flow of your article. Try putting them together in a fact box. For example, you might be writing about the great Barrier Reef and how visitors can see it while scuba diving, sailing over it in a glass bottom boat or even low-level flying.

A fact box can contain: details on flight information, package holidays, web sites, cost of local accommodation from five-star hotels down to bed and breakfast, the price of a meal out for two in a modest restaurant, what shopping bargains are to be had locally, the climate at various times of the year, places of nearby particular interest to see, what insurance is desirable and a few hints on dealing with the locals.

Apart from providing worthwhile up-to-date information, if the editor passes your article to the layout artist he immediately has a colour panel to break up the text along with the pictures you supplied. You did supply pictures didn't you?

An article with illustrations has double or treble the chances of acceptance. Make sure they are good. A picture of you on a camel with a knotted handkerchief on your head will not sell many magazines and one of the Eiffel Tower will not strike a note of originality.

Contrary to popular opinion editorial offices do take care with copy sent to them but items get lost. Paper clips have a habit of mating with the wrong mss, juniors shattered by the breakdown of their first love affair put things into the wrong envelope and our expensive Royal Mail occasionally gets things wrong.

Do not send originals. Keep a copy of everything and include a schedule of what you send. Do caption your illustrations clearly but not in ball-point pen on the reverse. Write or type the captions on an adhesive label and fix them to the back of a photograph with your name and address and the title of your article.

Put yourself in the editor's chair. What do you want? Ideally you will want something which is original and topical. Topicality is essential for many magazines hence you must work ahead. It's no good sending a Christmas feature to an editor in November.

Something on Valentine's Day will need to be despatched during November for a February magazine. Newspapers have shorter deadlines and you could try a Valentine's Day article a month ahead of the day.

As an editor you will also want to surprise your readers. Every editor wants a reader to feel that at least one article or feature in his publication is worth the cover price of the magazine alone.

Before you began to write your piece you had a sheaf of notes and references and did you also have five or six markets in mind for your article?

You will have studied those markets for length, and analysed everything about them. You will also have studied parallel titles in the United States, Canada, Australia and other English speaking countries.

Find out how editors like to receive copy: on a CD, or via email, or on a floppy with a hard copy. Do they like pictures via email?

There is no reason why you should not sell your article five or six times. That is a professional way to work. Never sit down to write a feature without having a firm idea of where you are going to place it.

La Charette *(Pat Rowlands)*

This was an enjoyable piece which should find a ready market in any Welsh newspaper or magazine and be interesting even to people outside the hillsides and valleys. There were plenty of facts and colour to spare. It would benefit from light editing and the style might be too colloquial for some tastes but that is easy to remedy. FIRST

Poperinghe *(Diane Wilson)*

A good, tightly controlled piece of writing, factual and information. Although much has been written about these times, the hardships of World War I and Tubby Clayton the personal experience of the author helps the perspective. Where it could be improved is by introducing some well-known personality or soldier who spent some time there. Perhaps someone decorated for bravery, or even an author like Wilfred Owen. For example, did Canadian or American troops visit Poperinghe?

One way to judge a piece of this nature is to try to select a market. In this case *This England, Saga* and *Choice* come quickly to mind. SECOND

Where Only Birds Could Fly *(Pam Dickinson)*

A well-written piece long on description, short on facts. Travel articles must impart information and I refer you to the general notes. If your piece is so lyrical that it makes people want to visit the location you must give basic information on how to get there and the cost. The piece could be sharpened by skilful editing. Beware of "fine writing," and using three words where one will do. THIRD

The Calendar *(Sue Round)*

This was a short, neatly researched article of the type that used at one time to be the bread and butter of general interest magazines from *Readers' Digest* down to *Answers* or *Titbits*. There is still a market for this feature and a leap year might give an element of topicality to improve its chances. FOURTH

John Jenkins

Judge's report
Best novel

First: **Our Lady Of The Petty Thieves** *(Lilian Ledger)*
This novel is instantly engaging. Immediately the reader is drawn into the tragicomic world of a range of well-drawn characters who would be perfectly at home in a northern soap (perhaps the writer would consider this!), but real people in whom we can believe and sympathise with. The writer's 'take' on the world is perceptive, sharp, witty, cynical and light-hearted by turns, achieving the subtle but powerful effect of seeing poignancy and humour among ordinary and sometimes rather meaningless lives. All of this is laced through with rich threads of irreverence – highlighted and symbolised by the title – which might offend some people but delight the trickster in most of us. The writing is clean and unfussy; the dialogue masterful, the author's commentary on the world (s)he explores sparkling with closely observed but not overdone detail. This entry was just superb.

Second: **Driving Force** *(Dee Weaver)*
A crisply-written synopsis, of just the right length and amount of detail, leads into equally elegantly constructed and pacy opening chapters. These swiftly evoke the novel's two main characters, Hugh and Ailsa, and establish the delightful contrasts and tensions between them (not least of which is a simmering sexual tension, a powerful draw to sustain the reader's interest). Furthermore, the writer deftly moves between these characters' point-of-view, so that although we can recognise their shortcomings, we also find them likeable and believable. The writing of this work is unselfconscious and accomplished. Vivid stylistic touches and evocation of little details leap off the page, as for example on P3 where the author draws our attention to a painting in Sinclair's office, 'a large abstract canvas fizzing with colour.' That *fizzing* attests to the quality of this work and its well-deserved high placing in the competition.

Third: **In Chain** *(Helen Culnane)*
This is a readable and highly entertaining period drama filled with warm and sympathetic characters with whom we quickly identify (Personally I was reminded of the TV drama *Upstairs Downstairs* – and I say this as a compliment to the quality of the author's vision and writing skill). The reader is quickly drawn in to the world of the story, the area around Elgin in Scotland in the 1910s, and made to feel at home there. The story moves along at a comfortable pace, never rushed, never dawdling, and remains 'buoyant' due to clear insights into the time, place and manners of the people. The use of dialect is

sure and unforced but not overdone, and the narrative twinkles with light touches of humour which contrast with the broader comedy of, for example, Dolly dealing effectively with Jean's would-be suitor (Pp 21-22), and with moments of poignancy, as when Alice is given her basket chair (P14). For me the defining feature of the excellence of this work is that I wanted to read the rest of the manuscript!

Fourth: **Cauldron** *(Sally Spedding)*

My first impression was that this story was 'a good potboiler.' The writer has a clear sense of purpose and a strong working knowledge of how the genre (crime/mystery) should be constructed. Delightfully (and with a sense of mischief I wonder?), the story is set in the literary world of Booker Prize nominations and the fierce air of competitiveness and ratings-grabbing kudos that these seem to generate in the publishing world. The plot, as laid out in the synopsis, is complex as befits this kind of fiction, but the reader is led by the author's steady hand through the opening chapters and never once feels lost or confused. Occasional heavy-handedness in trying to evoke atmosphere (such as the slightly purple prologue) is easily forgiven in light of beautifully elegant touches, as when Cindy, in making a phone call, 'could hear a dog barking in the distance and a woman telling it to belt up or else.' The use of such details as these is a true mark of high quality authorship, insofar as the reader's imagination is engaged to fill out the rest of the picture. While *Cauldron* may not win a Booker Prize, it might well land its author a well-deserved publishing deal.

Steve Bowkett

Judge's report

Best mini-tale

This year's mini-tale competition was open only to those who attended the Open Festival of Writing. The opportunity was there for writers to craft their piece before the weekend itself, but many entries were obviously put together at the last minute.

With a 5pm deadline and an announcement of the winner due to be made during the Awards Ceremony, time was not available for a lengthy judging. However, as the judge, I felt I was entitled to expect short, sharp observations on life which grabbed my attention.

The fact is that while one story may have been more carefully constructed, or another perfect in grammar or style, I was looking, as I assume most judges are, for something with a "Wow!" factor.

In a piece of no more than one hundred words, a writer's best option is, perhaps, to introduce a twist in the tale.

There were many of these in the fifty to sixty entries, but the majority unfortunately signalled the end or were too clichéd to be different.

I chose *My best friend's secret* because I liked the twist, the somewhat controversial story line – I'm afraid lesbian relationships are not prevalent on the shores of Bridlington Bay, and if they are I haven't yet been involved.

It is easy to say that "Tony" is not the feminine spelling, and that it should have been "Toni," but who can tell with names these days?

Mike Wilson

<u>Judges' report</u>

Best group anthology

The anthology that we decided was the overall winner was *A Galaxy of Rhyme and Prose* by the Friday Writers' Circle. This anthology was liked by the entire panel and everyone liked it for different reasons. The writing felt totally natural throughout and was a pleasure to read. Again, the diversity of topics covered and writing forms were wide, but the difference was in the writing itself. The pieces seemed the right length to engross the reader in the subject matter without dragging. The characters or occasions were not only described but emoted, giving the reader a much stronger feeling towards the work. You became involved in the story or poem you were reading and it became more than simply words on a page.

All the work we saw was with merit and I hope you all continue to enjoy not only your own writing, but take stimulation and pleasure from the writers you work with.

Pauline Haughey and Team
The Arts Centre, Washington

NAWG Annual Creative Writing Competition 2003

The full results (runners-up in alphabetical order, not order of merit. See Judges' Comments)

*Category 1: **Best Free Verse Poem*** (judged by Stephen Wade): Winner: **Dorothy Nelson** *(Afternoon)*, Ashton in Makerfield Writers & Literary Group. *Runners-up:* Jean Beard *(Social Outcast)*, Associate Member; John Lindley *(The House Where The Muse Is Kept)*, Congleton Writers' Forum; Aarti Narayan *(UFP)*, Associate Member.

Highly Commended entries (four): W. S. Allen *(The Sea Coal Gatherer)*, A Hartlepool Writers' Group; Elizabeth Parish *(Asylum Seeker)*, Salford Women Writers; Asit Maitra *(My Mole)*, Write Away Group Newcastle; Jean Corbett *(Dad)*, Write Away Group Newcastle.

*Category 2: **Best Formal Poem*** (judged by Alison Chisholm): Winner: **Diane Impey** *(Eating Songbirds)*, Market Rasen Writers; *Runners-up*: Joan Condon *(Nicking Knickers)*, Associate Member; Deborah J. Gotch *(Superman)*, Women Writing Southside; John Statham *(Checkmate)*, Alsager Writers' Circle.

Highly Commended entries (three): Anna Longshaw *(Secret Places)*, Alsager Writers' Group; Joy C. Swan *(Autumn Sonnet)*, Newcastle College Hexham; Colin Ferguson *(Sweethearts Forgot)*, Thames Valley Writers.

*Category 3: **Best Short Story*** (judged by Lynne Patrick): Winner: **Irene Black** *(Street Talk)*, Guildford Writers' Circle; *Runners-up*: Chris Barker *(Priced Above Rubies)*, Kessingland Writers; Ghislane Davies-Goff *(The Gift)*, Barrack Road Writers; John Statham *(Spaced Out)*, Alsager Writers' Circle.

Highly Commended entries (three): Margaret Cronin *(The Perfect Fare)*, Camberley Writers' Circle; Eileen Dowsing *(Turbulence)*, Kessingland Writers; Joyce Reed *(Stickleback)*, Marple Writers' Workshop.

*Category 4: **Best Novel*** (judged by Stephen Bowkett): Winner: **Lilian Ledger** *(Our Lady of The Petty Thieves)*, Dunholme Writers' Group; *Runners-up*: Helen Culnane *(In Chain)*, Cambridge Writers; Sally Spedding *(Cauldron)*, Barrack Road Writers; Dee Weaver *(Driving Force)*, Airedale Writers' Circle.

There were no Highly Commended entries in this category.

Category 5: Best Non-Fiction Article (judged by John Jenkins)*:* Winner: **Pat Rowlands,** *La Charrette,* Carmarthen Writers' Group; *Runners-up*: Pam Dickinson *(Where Only Birds Could Fly)*, Wilmslow Writers; Sue Round *(The Calendar)*, Worcester Writers' Circle; Diane Wilson *(Poperinghe in World War I and Today)*, Free Spirit Writers.

Highly Commended entries (four): Maureen M. Toyn, *The Reluctant Housewife*, Wyndham Writers' Group; Joyce Reed, *Occupied Territory*, Marple Writers' Workshop; Barbara Klempka, *Rag Bo'*, Airedale Writers' Group; Mavis Bailey, *Tobago Jewel of the Carribean*, Writers' Reign.

Category 6: Best Sit-Com (judged by Ken Rock): Winner: **Peter Rolls** *(The Grass Is Greener)*, Camberley Writers' Circle; *Runners-up*: John Birch *(No Place For Heroes)*, Carmarthen Writers' Circle; Lilian Ledger *(Delusions of Darcy)*, Dunholme Writers' Group; Sangie Sen *(A House In The Country)*, Harrow Writers' Circle. There were no Highly Commended entries in this category.

Category 7: Denise Robinson Trophy for Best Group Anthology (judged by Washington Arts Centre Staff): Winner: **The Friday Writers' Circle** *(A Galaxy of Rhyme and Prose)*; Runners-up: Greenfield Writers Group *(As Writers Reign)*; Kessingland Writers *(Writers Blocks)*; Alyn Writers *(Dreaming)*.

Highly Commended entries (two): Burton Poets and Writers *(Reflections Across The River)*; Writers' Block *(Figures in a Landscape)*.

This year's Mini-Tale competition was available only to those attending the Festival. The winner was Catherine Cooper, while runners-up were Dorothy Cooke, Ann Revill and Jo Sadler.